WE THE PEOPLE

Also by Harry Moore

What He Would Call Them
Time's Fool: Love Poems
Retreat: A Way Forward
Bearing the Farm Away
Beyond Paradise: The Unweeded Garden
Broken and Blended: Love's Alchemy

WE THE PEOPLE

Confessions
of a
Caucasian Southerner

Harry Moore

Poems

Broadstone

Copyright © 2024 by Harry Moore

Library of Congress Control No. 2024938624

ISBN 978-1-956782-75-2

Design by Larry W. Moore

Cover photography by the author

Broadstone Books
An Imprint of
Broadstone Media LLC
418 Ann Street
Frankfort, KY 40601-1929
BroadstoneBooks.com

Contents

Prologue: Remembering Home

Ars Poëtica: What to Make of It / 3
Musing on Good Friday / 5

Part I
The Town: Fame and Infamy

Birds of a Feather / 9
Herman Shaw (I) / 11
The Study: Bad Blood / 13
Confession: Only in Remembering / 15
Herman Shaw (II) / 16
The Town / 18

Part II
The Farm: What We Didn't Know We Knew

Related / 23
Where Are You Coming From? / 24
By Any Other Name / 25
What's in a Name? (I) / 26
Cliché / 27
Dogs / 28
The Shadow / 29
The Times / 30
Our Places / 31
Trust (I) / 32
Lily Byrd / 33
Emory / 34
Debt / 35
Why GP Cries / 37
Trust (II) / 39
Fathers and Sons / 40
Privilege: Our Own Laws / 42

PART III

THE PAST: WHAT WE LEARNED

Dark Past / 47
Isham's Will / 48
Inventory: Ransom's Estate / 49
Ghosts (I) / 51
Ghosts (II) / 52
A Peculiar Institution / 54
Reparations / 55
Man-Price / 56
How Much Is Enough? / 57

PART IV

NEW EARTH: CREEPING TOWARD JUSTICE

A New Earth: 1955 / 61
Change / 63
What's in a Name? (II) / 64
Communion / 66
A Dangerous Journey / 67
Just Some Human Sleep / 68
Revive Us Again / 69
Barbershop / 70
Hands (I) / 71
Hands (II) / 73
A Great Country / 74
Micro-Aggressions: You People / 75
Members Only / 76
A Monumental Warning / 77
Micro-Civilities: A Little Leaven / 79
Micro-Civilities (II) / 80
Micro-Civilities (III) / 81
Micro-Civilities (IV) / 82
Diversity / 83
Taking a Stand / 86

Part V
Waking Up: What We Saw

The Jig Is Up / 89
It's Systemic / 91
It's (Not) Racial / 92
It's Theory / 93
It's Critical / 95
It's Racial: Sticks and Stones / 96
It's a Choice: E-motion / 98
Greed and Grace / 99
We the People / 100

Epilogue: Maybe This Time

Peculiar Customs / 103
Hope / 104
Maybe this time / 105

Notes / 108
Acknowledgments / 110

Prologue:

Remembering Home

Ars Poëtica: What to Make of It

English *poem* is from the IE base **kwei-*,
to heap up, build; *art* is from **ars-*, to join,
fit together; and *make* is from **maĝ,*
to knead, press, stretch.

It is, after all, work—*opus, oeuvre*—
energy expended, stitching and unstitching,
harder than scrubbing cobblestones
in Yeats's kitchen.
                    It drags backyard daisies
from the flowerbed, rocks from the corner
where the bulldog's ashes lie, wood blocks
the roofers left, wisteria shoots snaking up
the crepe myrtle trunk by the gate—piles,
joins till they make a bridge to a rural past,
a weatherboard house resting on stacks
of flat stones, with a tin top, a dead father
the biscuit maker. Relentless till everything
fits.
            Pacing planted cotton fields
in April, he scratched up random seeds
to check for sprouting, baked thick
pones of water-and-meal dog bread
for Alec, Lawyer, and Nell, who ranged
over piedmont hills on Saturday nights
baying after gray and red foxes. He sat
fence-post straight on his roan walking horse,
took up fishing in Saugahatchee Creek
after deep wheezing pulled him from
cotton and corn fields. Knowing
King James by heart, he bandied verses
with all comers in homes and on streets,
the battle thinning and weakening
under the weathering years.
                            With the
hands and hairy forearms of a farmer,

3

we make the world, heaping, kneading,
pressing, stretching, till it rises before us
like bread from a familiar oven.

MUSING ON GOOD FRIDAY

< IE base *sekw-, to see, say,
  note, show, observe, tell

Seeing is *saying*, the name
etching the image, first iris
of the season, purple, drenched
with overnight rain beside
a beaten yellow pansy and
red upthrust amaryllis bud.

You seek a shape you can
claim: sparrows chittering
on the tool shed roof, two
starlings and a male cardinal
with dark mask pecking
the wet grass, a rabbit
hopping by the back gate,

the large-potted schefflera
by the fence lugged out from
winter refuge on the sun porch
for its twentieth year—a gift
at your mother's funeral from
the shy centerfielder your daughter
dated but did not marry.
                      Nursed
out of cold and back into spring
sun year after year, it is a life
she had that you must guard—
the tall, lithe limbs, playing
basketball, the sassy humor,
bedrock loyalty, backstraining
cotton mill work, wheezing
bone-brittle days near the end.

You owe her food, clothes
she bought, love, devotion

Atlas couldn't lift, layers
of quilts in the cold winter
farm house, life and laughter
blooming year after year
in the large crabapple by the
back fence,
                    a dome of bees
buzzing like some spring
heaven you and your brother
raced toward, breathing
the tree's sweet blossoms
as fig and black walnut
budded and sparrows fussed
in the chinaberry by the well
and redbirds whistled and the
greening fescue and bermuda
world opened beyond the
pasture fence, and you leapt
as if none of you would ever die.

Part I

The Town:
Fame and Infamy

BIRDS OF A FEATHER

> *Segregate,*
> lit., to set apart from the flock
> < L *se-*, apart (see SECEDE)
> + *grex*, a flock

My happy rural childhood was laced
with fears of Russian bombs, jets
rumbling high overhead from Gunter
and Maxwell in Montgomery,

leaving puffy contrails, jolting us
with sonic booms that shook our
quiet world. We had no idea that
during the last big war a thousand

black airmen, twelve miles from
our unpainted weatherboard house,
trained to make our world safe—
Red-Tail Angels, Lonely Eagles, or,

to the Germans, Black Bird Men; no
idea that over Sicily, Tunisia, the Great
Sea as wingmen to lofty bombers they
flew thousands of sorties, shot down

hundreds of enemy planes, took out
a destroyer—no idea that many died,
many earned Purple Hearts, Silver
Stars, Distinguished Flying Crosses,

that their unit was cited for outstanding
performance and extraordinary heroism.
We were not surprised to learn they
trained in segregated barracks, separate

as one hand from another, and that they
came home to segregated restaurants,

schools, water fountains, public restrooms.
It all seemed as natural as cotton

chopping in spring, tart muscadines
hanging from a tall hickory in fall, like
a flock of geese flying south in winter,
arrow sharp in their tight v-formation.

Herman Shaw (I)

Sunday nights after church we crowded
into our '52 Ford pickup and drove
a basket of crumpled dirty clothes to
Mrs. Shaw's house—work and school
denims, tee-shirts, Mother's blouses
and skirts for her second shift mill job,
pullovers for my brother and me.

At the door of their long frame house,
still in her Sunday dress, Mrs. Shaw took
this week's basket and gave us last
week's stack—clean, folded, starched,
creased—with a clear air of equal
exchange as she took the dollars from
my mother's hand.
                        Two miles north
of us—across County Road 49, beyond
Mrs. Claudie Golden's shack of a store
where on weekday afternoons the bus driver
let us off to buy nickel ice cream cones—
they had their world, we ours, and we
only met in passing.
                        Of an age with my father,
Mr. Shaw was tall, reserved, driving
his dark Buick past our house with
polite nods.
                        How could I know he
was valedictorian of his high school class,
that he studied Latin, algebra, physical
geography, and European history, that
he wanted to go to college and major in
engineering but stayed with their farm,
without resentment, at his father's insistence—
that he would see his own son and daughter
through college, selling a cow to pay tuition,

that he built with his own hands the white house
with dark trim where they lived?
                         How could I know
that twenty years before I knew him, his
money as thin as the piedmont soil he
grew cotton and corn in, he answered
an ad at a local church and—with full faith
in his government and in medical science—
signed on with the U.S. Public Health Service
for free health care? How was he to know?

The Study: Bad Blood

Syphilis or the French Disease,
    title of a poem (1530)
    by Girolamo Fracastoro:
    after the hero, *Syphilis*

Of uncertain origin, no
respecter of persons, named
for a shepherd who angered
a god.
                    Demon bug
riding the tenderest touch, the
crass selling of a woman's body,
or violent soldiers' rape.
                    Pustules
like leprosy, so repulsive every
nation blamed an enemy: the
French Disease, Neopolitan,
German, Polish. To the Muslim:
Christian or Hindu; to the Hindu:
Muslim—fear, outrage rarefied
into tribal hate.
                    Subversive, latent
for years, decades, then virulent,
attacking heart, nerves, brain,
sanity, eyes—blinding, killing
helpless newborns or leaving
the tell-tale collapsed saddle nose.

Treated with bland plant broth
or toxic mercury or arsenic that
wracked the body it should save.

In the first grip of our country's
Depression, how could a public-
minded project to treat young
Negro men
                    go so wrong?

How could a white doctor, in language
ripped free of all conscience, explain
that "the proper procedure is the . . .
observation of the Negro men . . .
with the idea of eventually bringing
them to autopsy"?

                    What hideous
assumptions about Negro men? What
cauterizing of moral sensibilities after
penicillin might have cured them all?

What sustained deception as annual
placeboes were doled out for "bad blood"?

What strained and intricate vigilance to
ensure that local doctors did not treat
the infected men?
                    What denial, guilt, shame,
local and national complicity, forty years in,
when a reporter blew the lid?
                    *Insidious infection
in the Body Politic, latent, pervasive; secrecy
blinding us all, subverting sanity and justice;
untreatable till decades of leg-wearying work
by local lawyers expose the open sores
and we confess.*

CONFESSION: ONLY IN REMEMBERING

< L *confessus* . . . < *com-*, together
+ *fateri,* to acknowledge; akin to *fari,*
        to speak: see FAME

Confession *speaks,* says the words, bodies
forth and faces the inexcusable wrong,
the infamy. It does not say *if* or *I didn't
mean,* only we did this, we were wrong,
we are sorry, what can we do?

Confession is communal. It speaks *to* and
with someone, goes on record, invites
judgment, wants to repair what's torn,
heal what's wounded.
                          With the old man
at his elbow, other survivors facing him,
the President acknowledges forty twisted,
wrong, wrung, silent years, a shameful past
we dare not forget.
                          Hundreds were hurt,
lied to, betrayed under a medical banner,
under the stars and stripes of our democracy,
a disease, like a toxic well we knew
they drank from, allowed to run its course
so we could study it—an outrage, deeply,
profoundly wrong.
                          The clock won't stop,
let alone turn back. We can't erase the pain,
the eyes gone blind, brains confused, blank,
wives infected. What's done is done.
                                              But
we can break the silence, speak, stop turning
our heads away, refusing to look. We can
see what we've done. So sixty-five years
too late, we the people confess the wrong,
the inhuman deed, the sustained deception.
It was shameful, and we are sorry. What
can we do?

Herman Shaw (II)

"After such knowledge, what forgiveness?"
T. S. Eliot

Forty years north of Golden's Store and
Simmons Chapel A.M.E. Zion Church,
he is at the White House—one of eight
survivors of the infamous Tuskegee
Syphilis Study.
   At 95, tall, quiet spoken,
he is direct and clear. What's done cannot
be undone. We were all hard-working men,
he says, citizens—men, not boys. We were
treated like guinea pigs. Some died, some
went blind, others insane; some families live
forever knowing the suffering and death
they saw was preventable. The deception
eroded faith in government and medical science.

Then, remarkably—not even pivoting, since
a peace he arrived at years ago has ridden
in the calm voice from the start—he says it's
never too late to forgive, never too late
to heal, restore trust.
   He is an American,
he says, and wants us to be one America,
black, red, white together, trusting each other,
caring for each other, never allowing such
a tragedy again. As of now, he says, he
has forgotten about it.
   Is this possible—after
the ships, the auction blocks, the war,
a state constitution bloated and tangled
to block freedom at every turn, lynchings
to breed fear and cowering—when we
the people have done our worst, treating
our neighbors like rats in a cage—is it
possible to follow this elderly man with

fine walnut skin, this praying man, into
good will, gratitude, humility—into
forgiveness and renewed trust?

The Town

Tuskegee, Muskhogean tribe,
   possibly meaning "warrior"

Fifteen miles and a world away, it
was urban, crowded, exotic,
                              where
my cousin lived in a red brick two-story
that was also a jail, the second-floor
gallows still intact.
                    He, the sheriff's son,
and I roamed freely, swimming in the city's
whites-only pool, talking with friends
at the Dairy Queen, driving with black
trustee Noah to feed and ride a horse
on some farm my uncle had bought, or
furtively and brazenly tailing unsuspecting
shoppers in Alley Mercantile or Lewis
Drugs on the square, relishing their
nervous glances, then gaining a roof
to stare over the parapet at busy streets
and sidewalks, a domain we moved
free and safe in.
                In the square's center,
a stone Confederate soldier said to
Honor the Brave towered fifty feet
over a park created for white people.
Resting the butt of his musket on
the ground and holding the barrel
in both hands, he faced north, ever
vigilant against any threat to our
Southern ways.
              The Institute,
in its trimmed, prosperous neighborhood,
was distant, mysterious, something I
learned about later when the bookmobile
from Dadeville brought brown hard-back

biographies of B. T. Washington and
G. W. Carver to my county school—

with no clue about president Moton,
authors Ellison and Murray, airmen
Roberts and McGee, pianist Teddy
Wilson, architect W. S. Pittman,
or activist Amelia Robinson.
                              What
were we to make, in our child's play,
of black people who were doctors
and professors and scientists—where
they dressed in suits and Sunday dresses
to shop on town square?
                              How could
we know where we were headed as we
mounted our horses and rode out of town
toward a rented barefoot farm fifteen miles
and a world away?

Part II

The Farm:
What We Didn't Know We Knew

RELATED

With four grandparents, nine uncles,
nine aunts and twenty-three first cousins

who swam with my brother and me
in Gantt's Mill Pond, played baseball

on our homemade pasture field, and
shot squirrels and doves with us in fall

I knew family ties were strong and close
as a crowded pew in church on Sunday.

So one day when I was six and we drove
on our dirt road past the dogtrot house

of black neighbors Aunt Susie and Uncle
Jim Wright where my parents and brother

lived before I was born, I asked if they were
really kin to us. We had some laugh at that.

WHERE ARE YOU COMING FROM?

When my father called on a neighbor's
party-line phone, Tuskegee Institute sent
vets at no cost to treat the heifer whose
first calf was too big to birth.

Polite, professional, in white coats,
they slogged through cow-lot mud
to a stall beside our tin-top log barn
where the heifer bellowed,

and in a strenuous, bloody operation
that stretched through hours,
sacrificed the calf to save the cow.

Grateful, we thanked these black doctors
genuinely, politely, as they took leave—
noting their light color and crisp speech,
wondering where they might be from.

By Any Other Name

When we sang the child's rhyme
Eeenie Meeney Miney Mo to
pick who went first
                    and when
we named a Brazil nut or a golden
flower with dark navel
                    and when
we found a mama dog and four pups
in a box by our gravel road
                    and I
begged till my father said we
could keep them
                    and the dark gaunt
mother stayed with us and ranged
the hills in relentless pursuit of rabbits,

it seemed only natural we would
call her a Latin name meaning *black*
that also described our neighbors,

a word that crept into our speech
like kudzu climbing a fence post—
thoughtless as *hickernut, lighterd knot,*

or *roasnears*—unnoticed till cows ate
the tough, hairy leaves and vines and
the milk was rank for weeks on end.

WHAT'S IN A NAME? (I)

Moor < ME *More* < OFr *More, Maure*
    < L *Maurus*, a Moor, Mauritanian
      member of the Muslim people of
   mixed Arab and Berber descent living
          in North Africa

Under summer sun my blond brother
burned brown as some colored faces

we knew, though not as dark as Moors
we might have been named for—

a swarthy heathen hue our pale European
neighbors hated and feared and fought

for centuries—a culture that arrogant
Greeks called Berber, barbarous,

barbarian, mocking the words they
could not understand.

                    We parched
and ate *goobers* on our farm, boiled

and fried *okra* every summer day,
wondered at *gumbo* in a distant city,

scoffed at *voodoo*,
                        little knowing

that on planet Earth we all crawled from
an African cradle, dark pigment spreading

around the globe, thinning and fading
under a weak northern sun till now we

deny our own.

Cliché

Too young and back-country to
know a slur when it screamed,

I chuckled outside the circle
of men at my uncle's Pure station

when he quoted the mythical maid,
"I spits in greens and cabbages

when I cooks them"—with no clue
the walls around us would tumble

when some reckless and courageous
prophet blew his trumpet.

Dogs

Everybody on our winding
dirt road knew our hounds,
curs, bulldogs, and collies

didn't like black people and
kept them from the yard
except to work for us.

When I was a toddler, they
said, and straddled our brindle
Bully, banging his head

with a hammer, he merely
ducked, cringed, would
never harm me,

                but when
my keeper, Sally, reached
to pick me up, he leapt

for her throat, they said. Even
he knew the secret script.

The Shadow

When I was three and we were
just back from Texas and lived

at Cousin Cromer's place in
two rooms with kerosene lamps

and an icebox cooled with blocks
of real ice from the ice plant,

and for a year my father farmed
the rocky hillside near the woods

where my brother, cousin Wilbur,
and I got poison oak from head to toe

and had to be bathed in calamine lotion,

one day the black maid walked

my brother and me down the dirt road
to Gooden's Store for Nehis, and we

laughed at how the maid's long shadow
moved as we walked and skipped and how,

when we stepped on her shadow, it
didn't hurt.

The Times

A child, I didn't know whether to laugh,
marvel at a culture so dark and near,

or weep for the young woman my
father said served him cold breakfast

four days running as he rose for
first shift at Mount Vernon Mills

before he discovered she could not
read the clock and in anxiety and

diligence was rising at 3:00 a.m.
to prepare him fatback, scrambled eggs,

biscuits, and coffee, knowing she
needed to please and being unsure

when the dawn would break.

Our Places

My father, oldest of eight, was
stern but not violent—laughed
with neighbors, prayed and sang
in church, paid the going wage

for field hands—but when
my brother, cousin, and I went
bird-thrashing with pine-pitch
torches one night in woods

below our house, and a carload
of people pulled their sedan into
a logging road in those woods,
with amorous intent,

my father stood behind the car
with his 12-gauge pump across
the crook of his arm and in
loud language he didn't use

in church told them they must
leave. Their boldness pushed
him past a limit, he said, his
boys in the very woods.

We laughed at how always
after that Timothy Washington,
when he drove past our house,
slowed his dark Mercury to

a crawl, nodded as deep as a
bow, and spoke to us. Nobody
needed to mention that Timothy
was black.

Trust (I)

When the preacher from out West
came to our little church to teach

us shape notes and *a cappella* singing,
and we sang "Trust and Obey" and

"When the Roll Is Called Up Yonder"
and my aunt and uncle's maid Mary

stole the preacher's wife's satin
Sunday dress, then returned it stained

and torn, we were shocked, we said.
She had picked cotton for us, almost

like family. Did this not prove you
couldn't trust them, no matter how

long you had known them or how
good you had been to them?

LILY BYRD

Her skin was pink, eyes blue,
hair wild and white, like a halo
around her albino face.
                              Her
undershot jaw worked busily as
she swept up at Parker's store,
oblivious to farmers coming
and going, lost in thoughts we
could not fathom.
                         We wondered
about her little box of a house in
a field past Wright's grist mill,
covered with red brick-siding,
spindly on columns of stacked stones.

And on dark nights when my brother
and our friend Larry conjured ghosts
and monsters, we trembled that we
might meet her on some murky,
moonless road,
                         afraid to imagine—
as she shambled towards us in untied
tennis shoes, mumbling a language
only she knew—what she might do to us.

EMORY

Famous with one name, like Homer
or Malcolm or Martin, pygmy-sized,
he manhandled the large suction pipe
at the gin as he moved it rhythmically
back and forth across packed loads
of cotton in one wagon after another,
his sculpted torso glistening black
with sweat as the pipe sucked locks
of cotton into the gin's roaring depths
where spinning, sharp interlocking teeth
ripped lint fibers from clinging seeds.

But when he walked Carrville streets, the
grace and strength leaked away, sagged
to a shuffling heel-dragging gait, eyelids
drooping, his tongue working among
random spaces between teeth as he talked
in jumbled tones with himself.
                              We knew
nothing of Emory's private life—where
his house was, how old he was, if he ever
went to school, what was funny to him, if
his parents hugged him when he was five
or thirteen, what he thought of himself—
only his public figure, like some boxer
or singer we might crowd around for
an autograph or picture.
                              One Sunday
in front of the white block church where
we had just sung hymns and unlocked
divine mysteries, my uncle, with a knowing
sidelong glance, accosted Emory, had him
pull from his pocket a dingy handkerchief
holding a long-rooted molar recently extracted.
Unperturbed, he met our chuckles all around
with a crooked smile and shuffled away
humming a tune none of us knew.

DEBT

     < L *debere*, to owe
   < *de-*, from + *habere*, to have:
             see HABIT

By July's end, with cotton laid by,
fields lush with green leaves, late
blooms, sleek tapered bolls swelling
toward bursting,
                            we drove east
in the Ford pickup, past Liberty City,
turned left toward the covered bridge
at Gold's Mill
                         and pulled into
a hard-beaten yard under tall pecan trees
and a thick water oak, where barefoot
black children swarmed from the gray
weatherboard house, scattering chickens
and two skinny dogs, crowding around
the truck's open window, one boy
asking for a nickel.
                              Then,
in an old dance we didn't know we knew,
my father loaned a man and two or three
women five or ten dollars each.
                              We knew
zilch of plantation life—I was furious
years later at books that equated the South
with patrician planters, a world as foreign
to us as Detroit or New York—and twelve
or fifteen bales of cotton were my father's
income for a whole year.
                              But on our little
stage we played our age-old parts: weeks
from now when the cotton stood tall and
bare and white, the dollars we loaned
would draw these men and women—sure

as a tether tied to their waist—to our field
to work off the debt.

                                        If they
owed us, they would do our bidding and
stay in their place.

Why GP Cries

1954

Beneath seething August heat
bolls of cotton crack, then burst
in fluffy locks, green leaves twist,
turn brown and fall. Black faces glisten
as workers bend to knee-high stalks,
plucking the soft fiber from prickly burrs,
packing handfuls into the canvas sack they drag
till it's strutted, then dumped on croaker sheets,
tied and weighed at day's end,
three cents a pound. Ice cubes clink
in gallon water jugs passed round.

One year my father picked six bales
alone, he said, three hundred pounds a day,
hauled to gin on Saturday, while working nights
at Mt. Vernon Mills. At ten, I picked two hundred,
beaming before him as the stillyards leveled steady
beneath the hickory pole we held.

2022

My tears live close to home
these days, rising up unannounced when
Hallmark says my daughter
has me in her heart, when a grandson
takes the hard grounder and flings
the ball to first, or when Lear howls
over limp Cordelia, searching for her breath.
But most I weep when King's great dream
rolls in waves of shimmering August light
through fields where Ralph, Laura, Earl, Roy,

Hershel, Mattie, Pete, and Robert
lean dark to rows white for harvest.

The vial breaks, the fountains rise, and
I have no words but go by water.

Trust (II)

At Parker's store they mill about,
order lunch one item at a time—a chunk
of hoop cheese for five cents, sardines
or viennas or a slice of souse meat
for ten, soda crackers for another dime,
and a Royal Crown for a nickel—
laying change on the counter for each
item before melding into the crowd
to look for the next one.
                        With heads as
good for numbers as any clerk, are they
making sure they have enough money,
that they don't embarrass themselves,

or do they fear complex accounting
because some landowner once said to
their fathers or grandfathers in November
of a mediocre crop year
                        that after he
calculated the seed, the fertilizer, rent
for the shack they lived in, ginning fees,
use of a mule and farm implements,
allowing a modicum for their labor
planting, plowing, chopping, picking,

they still somehow owed him money,
their share of the six bales they harvested
not quite knocking off the debt?

FATHERS AND SONS

for Dozier Pryor

"Sometimes when I'm eating," he said,
"or sitting by the fire
I get up and go out in the yard
because I don't know if he's warm
or has anything to eat."

We sat on split-bottom chairs
before a fireplace where oak
and hickory smoldered on blackened firedogs
against the evening chill.
Under graying hair curled tightly
against his head, his face was lined
like oak leaves in December, dark
as the coffee I drank every morning
with biscuits dipped in cane syrup
before boarding the bus to the county school
five miles away. His full lips
worked nervously, hands turning
the felt hat on his lap.
He had not seen my father's black and tan foxhound
lost three days since in the Big Woods
but wouldn't we come in and sit a spell.
His boy had gone to the army last spring.

I had seen him ride by our house on Saturday mornings,
buggy wheels crunching the gravel road
behind the steady brown horse stepping
toward town six miles away.
Returning at dusk wrapped
in army overcoat and blanket
he bowed deeply with a courtesy
befitting the owner of his own home
who did not pick other men's cotton.
Now, in the room that smelled
of woodsmoke, lye soap, warm bodies,
and years of fatback, crackling bread,

greens, and sweet potatoes baked
slowly into its pine walls, he spoke,
"I can't eat when he's hungry, I can't rest
when he's tired and cold."

Korea and Topeka were far away.
Selma slept. Rosa waited
in the back of the bus.

On the hard clay road,
in the cab of the Ford pickup moving
past pines and scrub oaks toward
the black grammar school,
I searched my father's face
for words I could not see.

PRIVILEGE: OUR OWN LAWS

> < L *privilegium*, an exceptional law for
> or against an individual
> or a particular group
> < *privus*, PRIVATE + *lex*, law: see LEGAL

When I was six and Mother drove me to
County School in our boxy black Model-T,

I could enroll in first grade and sit and listen
to gray-haired Mrs. Cosby tell how the raccoon
jumped over the fire and got his black-ringed
tail,
                    but Roy Terrell couldn't.

After I stood by our house on Gantt's Mill Road
one morning and watched a game hen fly to
the top of a fence post and fight off a chicken hawk
while her biddies ran cheeping but safe,
                              I could
get on the black and yellow school bus driven by
our cousin Jessie Mack Webster and sit down by
Sammy Barrington and talk about Mickey Mantle's
and Larry Doby's baseball stats,
                    but Roy Terrell couldn't.

In third grade at the Halloween Carnival, I could
do the cake walk though it might be gambling and
pillow fight on a pole with Ernest Patillo whose
father ran the flour mill,
                    but Roy Terrell couldn't.

In sixth grade when Mrs. Mary Belle Howard
paddled my friend Joey because he said Yea Big Jim
after she had explained that Big Jim's opponent was
a Christian man and would make the best governor,
all the parents and teachers could vote for Folsom
or Faulkner, Ike or Adlai,
                    but Roy Terrell's parents couldn't.

When Roy rode by our house in the pickup with
his father, Johnny, and we nodded and waved, I didn't
know where he lived, where his parents worked, or
what they ate for breakfast or supper. I didn't think
much about Roy at all,
                        till one day when we were twelve or so
as our bus turned around at Wright's grist mill and
Roy and his friends were walking toward home after
being let off their own bus and we looked out the back
window at them,
                        he turned to us, clutched his crotch
with both hands and thrust his pelvis forward, a wicked
grin shaping his features.
                        Our burst of laughter covered
confusion and wonder. Was this brazen breach of black
and white decorum a playful overflow of youthful spirits?
Was it a reckless gesture of pubescent camaraderie
that made Janice Johnson blush in recognition as she
laughed?
                Or did Roy tap some anger in his bones that said
fuck all you uppity white kids looking down your nose?

PART III

THE PAST:
WHAT WE LEARNED

DARK PAST

At 90 my hardworking and good-humored
grandfather says his Irish great-grandfather
ran ships with human cargo till he was
lost at sea,
           and a cousin hints darkly
that this trafficker's son, our great-
great-grandfather, bought his first farm
in our county with dollars from men
and women he sold.
             Another patriarch
in my line willed people to his children
like kitchen utensils,
           and his intestate son
left them to be inventoried and valued
like mules and plowstocks.
              Where are
the sons and daughters of these bartered souls?
Have they clawed their way out of plantation
and sharecropper shacks, walled neighborhoods,
gotten past locked school doors, blocked
voting booths? Have they escaped burning
and hanging? Have they found a court that
sees them, hears their voice, a bank to stake
them a house where they want to live? Do
they know they can look straight on and
not avert their eyes? How can I know
they've found a new day?

Isham's Will

22 November 1844

To my son Ransom, I will and bequeath
the Mill Seat which he occupies
including the Mill Pond, say
three acres more or less.

To my son Asa
I give Sophia.

To my son Edward
I give Mary and Sam.

To my son Daniel
I give John and Harriet.

All my landed property I give
to my wife, Martha, during her life,
all my household and kitchen furniture,
all Plantation utensils, wagons, carts, etc.,
all stock, horses, mules, cows, hogs, etc.
together with all crops, corn, cotton. Also,
all the ready money which may be on hand.

To my son James
I give Sally and Marcus.

To my daughter Martha
I give Dolly and Frank.

To my son Benjamin
I give Henry, Peter, and Joanna
and sixty dollars besides.

Inventory: Ransom's Estate

30 May 1863

A full true and accurate appraisement
of the goods chattels moneys and
debts of said deceased:

One large ox wagon, one black mule
Bill, one sorrel horse Snake, six bee hives,
eighteen goats, Rachael a negro woman
and child Elizabeth, one stallion John

Baccus, one note from Gilbert Meecham
two hundred fifty dollars, insolvent.
Polly Ann a girl, George a boy, and
three hundred feet of lumber.

One gray horse Charley, one metal
clock, six hundred bushels of corn,
two hundred cans of lard. Zeke a man,
Abby a woman, Benny a boy, and Sam

an old man. Two hundred head of hogs,
eight chairs, one lot of carpenter's tools,
one cotton gin, two thousand shingles,
blacksmith tongs, anvil, and bellows,

and one wheat fan. Henderson a man,
Alex a boy, Frances a girl. One hack
and harness, one crosscut saw, three
bed quilts, one bedstead and furniture,

Ann and child Louisa. Eleven cows
and calves, one secretary and bookcase,
a dark mule old Kit, Louisiana Matilda
a girl, one bay mare Fanny, one short

double barrel shotgun, a loom, two
spinning wheels, eleven plow stocks,
Lucretia a girl, one small table, and
Esther an old woman valueless.

Ghosts (I)

Macon Telegraph, Nov. 5, 1831:
Sheriff's Sales, Houston County:
"Negro woman, Anna, 38 or 40 yrs.,
    ppty. of Levin F. Chain,
    fi fas of Moss & Cassiday."

Do farmers stand about the square on
this late fall day, talking rain and the last
scraps of cotton in soggy fields?
                            How
had the Irishman come by her before
losing legal claim? Had she ridden
the dark hold across an ocean, or was
she native?
                    Was she tall, and did her
coarse cotton dress hang loose on her frame,
and did a buyer squeeze her bare shoulder
and eye her rounded breast?
                            Did she
have a husband, someone who caressed
her, talked to her, held her in the night?

What work awaited her in field or kitchen?
What shack would she live in, what fire
kindle against the cold, what food at end
of day, what allotted shoes and clothes?

Would auctioneer, sheriff, buyers, sellers,
sit in church come morning—would they
sing of amazing grace, so glad to be found,
forgiven?
            And when some child of Anna's
now awakes in a room in Atlanta, Macon,
or Chicago, yawns, and walks to the kitchen
for coffee, with what fear does she move
into her November day?

Ghosts (II)

> *Macon Telegraph*, Nov. 5, 1831:
> Sheriff's Sales, Houston County:
> "Negro woman, Anna, 38 or 40 yrs.,
>   ppty. of Levin F. Chain,
>   fi fas of Moss & Cassiday."

Is this my Irish great-great-grandfather
who fought the British in 1812 and then
the Indians on all fronts—Southern born
while Washington led the new nation,

coming to Alabama four decades later,
buying the old home place at Walnut Hill,
siring fifteen children by two wives—
documented in all censuses, dying
a decade after Emancipation?

What was he up to, this elusive forebear,
this soldier, flitting across Georgia
in his thirties, trafficking in land grants
like horses he bought and couldn't feed,
one property after another sold by some
sheriff on courthouse steps for taxes
or legal claim? What kept this Captain
so busy he couldn't pick up letters
in Milledgeville and Columbus?

And was Anna one more property he
couldn't keep? Where was he that bustling
Saturday as she stood on the square waiting
to know her worth?
                    And when in age he knew
the comforts of wife and children's children,
of planting and harvest as he watched pickers
bending over the rows of cotton, did he ever
think of her?

What genes
from this restless, gun-bearing trader now
lurk in the cells of my being?

A Peculiar Institution

< L *peculium*, private property
    < *pecus*, cattle

Peculiar indeed. Not
particular, unique, special,

our very own Southern
arrangement, noble scheme

behind magnolias and tall
columns, heritage resting

on broad fields.
              Rather,
odd, strange, a system built

on human backs, herding
people like *pecus,* cattle,

guarding narrow *pecuniary*
interests, *peculating,* stealing

the dignity and freedom of
thousands who might have been

our neighbors. No better than
common greed and pride of place.

A real cottonmouth in our claims.

REPARATIONS

> < L *reparare* < *re-*, again
> + *parare*, to get ready, set in order

Repair: to put back in good condition
after damage, decay,
                              to mend
                    fix
                                        renew
restore
                    revive
                                        amend
make good
                    make amends
                                        make up for

set right
                    compensate for.

MAN-PRICE

OE *wergild* < *wer*, man + *geld*, price
In Anglo-Saxon law, a price paid by a person
who has killed another
to the family of the person killed,
to atone for the killing and avoid reprisals.

Is it after all Anglo-Saxon and not
African, this incursion of commerce
into the world of moral values, how
I should treat my neighbor?
                    Owe no man
anything but to love one another.
It's what we *ought* to do, *pay* respect
to all. It's our *duty*, an *obligation*
we are *obliged* to honor. We pay our
just *dues*, our *debt* to society when
we fail. Forgive us our *debts* as we
forgive our *debtors*.
                    In court, we
seek *damages*, actual and punitive,
each life, every limb, organs, eyes,
ears, assigned a *value*.
                    How much would
Anna's descendants have earned had
she been free, educated, encouraged?
What skills, professions for Isham's
Sophia, Sam, Harriet, John, Joanna—
what retirement for Ransom's old
and valueless Esther?
                    What penalty
for chains, whips, ships, auctions—
human lives snuffed out without legal
consequence? What *payback* for dozens,
hundreds, thousands? What currency
for such debt? Do we add interest?

What confession counts the cost?

How Much Is Enough?

"The man hath penance done,
And penance more will do"
        (Coleridge,
"Rime of the Ancient Mariner")

If I locked my son outside,
banished him from meals
till he was fourteen, would

I kill the fatted calf, add
mounds of potatoes, cakes,
when I finally welcomed him

to the family table? Would
I be worried he might get
an extra portion?

            If children
are abused by priests, uncles,
addicted parents, and I say

children's lives matter, does
that mean adults' lives are
less, and do not matter?

                If
one woman and another and
another are bruised, beaten,

kept at home in fear with
no money, and I say their
lives matter, does that mean

men are naught, no more
than a marauding lion
attacking a village?

                    If
George is choked, Ahmaud
and Trayvon shot, Tulsa's

Greenwood terrorized and
burned, and I say black lives
matter, who would think

white legacy students at Yale,
white policemen, white lawmakers,
white voters, Tulsa's white

Chamber of Commerce ever
did not matter?
                    Till

we have hungered outside
the door, been denied a seat
at the lunch counter, a desk

in a fully funded school, been
beaten in the street or shot
in our home, we should save

the quip about how much we
matter. We've hardly scratched
our towering debt.

PART IV

NEW EARTH:
CREEPING TOWARD JUSTICE

A New Earth: 1955

for Rosa Parks

After our pale fingers, and fingers
darker than our own, plucked the cotton
from the burrs, the stalks weathered

in the fields, through frost, freeze, thaw—
through hog-killing, crackling fireplaces,
cured ham, salted fatback, squirrels shot

from leafless hickories for pots of dumplings.
Then, in soggy, glaring, cold, windy March,
the massive stalk-cutter—a two-foot-thick

poplar log with rusty iron blades
along its length—rolled and bumped
behind mules along the cotton rows,

smashing stalks into segments, chopping
withered pursley, crabgrass, bull nettle,
cleaving earth, marking the field for fire,

flames spreading before a stiff breeze,
eating through stalks and dried grass,
pungent smoke rising toward some cosmic

conflagration St. Peter told us would
come, countryside and sky in flames,
a judgment settling all accounts, purging

tares, sawbriers, maypop vines, bitterweed,
tenacious bermuda, clearing the soil of clutter,
like gold cleansed of alloy, nothing left

but goodwill, courage, and kindness to all
alike—a new heaven and new earth—making
way for the steelbeam turning plow to rip

through ash, fling up the soil's dark underside
rich with promise for a new planting, for
a harvest like none we'd ever known.

Change

We all laughed and shifted with
uneasy virtue when my cousin

Larry at age three came inside
and wanted a popsicle for himself

and another for his little black friend
and when there was only one popsicle

sat with his friend on the front steps
taking turns licking the sweet grape ice

till it disappeared.

What's in a Name? (II)

    moor < ME *more* < OE *mor,*
     open, rolling wasteland, usually
   covered with heather, often marshy.
       < IE base **meri-*, sea,
  basic sense, "swampy coastland" (Brit.)

Nowhere near the coast, and with
kudzu for heather, we yet lived

on rolling piedmont hills sloping
toward the sea, swamps behind

and before, cottonmouths curled
beside alder-shaded brooks that

we called branches, like limbs
in someone's family tree.

         To the
City of Brotherly Love came James

and John, blacksmith and locksmith,
working for Mr. Penn, already Friends

or soon to be. Somewhere across
three centuries and five states, they

leapt from Quaker to Campbellite,
keeping a stark simplicity. Did some

inner glow yet burn, like a drop-down
bulb in the old farmhouse, when

my brother braved a draft board and
held his peace.

        And did some gene
yet linger in an inmost cell for a deeper

peace—a ripple, an echo, a whisper,
clarion blast from sea to sea, saying all

are equal, all free, that no one comes
to the back door hat in hand?

COMMUNION

In the plain white rectangular
church where we had found
the formula for salvation
everyone else missed,
                in a State
whose racist demagoguery
stifled like lung-choking mold
in a damp room,
                the congregants
did not question the motives of
a black family drawn to worship
with them.
                Instead, they
gave rides to Luke, wife Mattie,
and their two daughters, shaking
their hands, and
                when the grape juice
and unleavened crackers passed
around—like bread the slaves
in Egypt ate before the death
angel passed over them and slew
their oppressors—my parents,
aunts, uncles, cousins ate and
drank with Luke and his family.

If, as St. Paul said, there was neither
male nor female, Jew nor Greek,
bond nor free, then surely there was
neither black nor white.

A Dangerous Journey

In the year I lost my draft deferment
and taught five preps of high school English
at New Site School while writing a thesis

and carpooled twelve miles with Charles
and Rhonda from math and Julie from
fourth grade,
                        all went well
till Rhonda's husband and Julie's father
discovered Charles was black and their
wife or daughter some chilly October
morning
              might ride twenty minutes
alone in a car with a man they would
later sit beside in a faculty meeting,

and Julie and Rhonda bailed from
the car pool and I moved thirty miles
away to care for a sick father, and Charles
once more made the perilous journey
from home to work alone.

Just Some Human Sleep

1968

In my 8:00 a.m. senior English class
at New Site School, where the principal
walked the halls with a well worn
paddle protruding from his back pocket,

and I, erudite at twenty-four, praised
Wordsworth's lament for lost youth
and explained to eighteen-year-olds
how Keats would cease to be at twenty-five,

Joseph Burns, one of four black students
in a recently integrated class, sitting second
from front, behind blonde and diligent
Belinda Foshee,
                        nodded off repeatedly
during my learned lectures.
                        Startled by
my clever quip that he might like to join us,
Joseph came to me quietly after class to say,
as oldest of three in a house with only
his mother to provide, he worked nights
at Russell Mills to help out, getting off
at 7:00 a.m.
                        Thereafter in class, when
Joseph nodded, I would nudge him lightly
or just lead my young charges through
Shelley's exalted claim that poets really
make the laws of the world—and move
finally to the superb ending of Keats'
great ode where the dying poet finds
peace in a stubble field at sunset while
swallows gather and twitter and
everybody else moves on.

Revive Us Again

When, in the boll weevil town
where I first taught college,
our conservative church invited

their black brothers and sisters
from across town to a revival and
they came on a Thursday night,

a distant cousin of my father's
he had played in knee breeches with
sixty years before who was home

from Merchant Marine duty
took loud umbrage at this radical
mixing of races, ranting in spluttering

red-faced anger that he would
not go to such a church—observing,
on my later visit designed to renew

old family ties, that only South
Africa knew how to lock blacks
away for the animals they were—

and I, in shame and surprise let
his hard-edged voice scrape like
a rock against a raw nerve till

the tension subsided into strained
reminiscence and I fled into a world
I lacked courage to change.

Barbershop

While I sit dozing as the barber
I've gone to for 40 years
trims my thinning peppered hair
exactly to my likes
                   and in the
crowded room a man with set
jaw and narrow eyes complains
about an unfriendly neighbor
who won't keep his hedge cut

confiding with hardly a side
glance that this foul neighbor
is black
                 I bristle and
break his rant and say I thought
we had gotten past such slurs
and in any case I have grandchildren
the word insults.
                 When he sputters
and saves face by asking if he
can finish his story and in the shop's
tense silence I say sure,
                   no one screams
the enormity of this outrage.

Hands (I)

At the self-help Admissions monitor
in the college where I taught writing
for thirty years,
                my grandson's fingers
dart across the keyboard *first name*
last name address gender. At
race/ethnicity he clicks "nonhispanic,"
pauses, then adds "black/African American."

For his slender muscular body,
the fingers are long and graceful, as if
he might play the piano or pluck soft
locks of cotton from bolls in August
heat, like Pete, Jerry, Robert, and Ralph
in my childhood.
                In truth, his fingers
are more at home gripping a football
before he arcs it forty-plus yards
into a racing receiver's waiting hands,

or dribbling a basketball deftly into
a crowded lane, then bouncing the ball
past defenders to a lanky teammate for
a quick layup
                or feinting a drive
from the corner, stepping back, and
lifting the spinning ball twenty feet
into the basket for three points.
                When
he was five—in the hotel pool where
we'd gone to watch the Braves and Orioles
on a sweltering Fourth weekend—we
two played swim-as-far-as-you-can in
the pool's clear water.
                Over and over
he pushed hard from the concrete edge,

swimming toward me under water as
I backed deeper and deeper into the pool,
his brown hand blurred in the rippling liquid,
reaching for and grasping mine again
and again, before he burst the surface,
gasped for air, and flung water to the side
with a toss of his head.
                              Now, after riding
a culture of ease and athletics through
his senior year, sleeping here, there,
at his mom's, his dad's, at this or that
grandparent's house, at a coach's or
girlfriend's house, with classes lagging
before he sprinted for two months to get to
graduation, he's ready to walk.
                              We tell him
the world is open, he can do what he will—
teaching, coaching, barbering, the military.

Before such wide space, so many choices,
he hesitates, unsure of these strange waters.

Hands (II)

Had he been in my rural world when he
was five or eighteen, his fingers would not
have picked up a fork at my table, passed
a football or tossed a baseball with me.
They would not have reached for the knob
on my front door.
                  He would not have swum
with us in Caleebee Creek on summer days
when rain freed us from the field—leaping
twenty feet from the rusty iron bridge into
the icy current whose bottom we could not reach.

He would not have slept in a bed at our house,
borrowed my large black comb, or stowed
a toothbrush in my bathroom.
                    He would have
ridden the faded yellow bus to Wall Street
School, kept to his neighborhood beyond
the swamp behind our house. He would
have bent to loaded cotton stalks with
other field hands for days, weeks after I
opened books on a new year.

A Great Country

In an email from an accomplished friend,
retired Army, a man wants to sign his
dogs up for welfare:
                they are mixed in color,
the man says, unemployed, lazy, can't speak
English, have no frigging idea who their daddy is,
and expect him to provide food, housing,
and medical care.
             After the government,
of course, signs them up, the narrator's voice
in the beast fable says, "Damn, this is
a great country!"
                When I say
to my friend that I respect his politics but
wish to be spared such tripe,
                 he says
he didn't see any political overtones,
just thought the send-up was funny,

and that among the forty-eight people
I counted that he sent it to,
nobody else complained.

MICRO-AGRESSIONS: YOU PEOPLE

Once is accident
                or impulse

        twice a choice
                    we move forward in

        three times a habit
                    we need.

Four is character
                mustard on the shirt
                        that won't come out

a closing of the eyes
        tug at the ear
                when we lie.

MEMBERS ONLY

< IE *_mēmsro-_, var. of _mēmso_, flesh

We are all one body, the saint says,
though with many _members_. All is
not eye or ear, hand or foot. One bite
feeds all, one heart beats for all.
Individual, indivisible, one.
                                    But
the burly doorman draws the line,
only his own kind allowed to enter,
the invisible barrier thick as blood
and bone—thin as a porous _membrane_
between dark pigment and our fair
blue-eyed crowd.
                                Around
the hurtling earth, could we but see,
streams course like limpid veins. Our
grasping kind rose tree limb above
limb, arms swinging, legs leaping,
ears ringing with dawn's birdsong.

The chorus swells with many voices,
hands hold, fingers thread, feet walk
stride for stride. One flesh, one breath
on a pulsing planet. We are not
the club we wield.

A Monumental Warning

< L monumentum < monere, to warn, remind
     < IE base **men-*, to think > MIND
               See MONITOR

In the river town I came to forty years ago
to teach verbs, nouns, symbols, the way
words can sing or deceive,

                         a town leveled
in an uncivil war a century before I came—
houses smashed, hundreds dead, only the
pocked and riddled Bank Building left as
evidence—

                    a tall monument stands,
with Johnny Reb atop the column, clasping
the barrel of his upright rifle, his stained
and weathered face looking east.

The stone base bears a CSA flag and twin
inscriptions: "Lest We Forget" and "To
the Memory of Those Who Offered Their
Lives for a Just Cause, the Defense of
States Rights."

                         What word,
what *warning*, does this *monument* bring
to mind? Does this soldier in his slouch hat
yet *think* his cause just?

                         Or does he caution
across the century since his loyal daughters
lifted him high that he was conned, that
states' rights rhetoric cloaked the horrors
of human bondage—his vaunted heritage
no more than planters' pride and wealth?

Does he regret a war that killed 500 men
a day for four years, over half a million
dead, thousands buried without a name?

Does he see that human worth and dignity,
our nation's heritage, always trump custom
and money—that stripped of rank and wealth
and fear, we stand self-evidently equal before
an unbiased creator?
                    And does this soldier's
face that takes each day's new light now
offer hope—does he *monitor* our progress
as black, white, Hispanic, Asian citizens
move briskly past his base, bent on tag
or license renewal, appearance in some court,

headed toward the new courthouse built
without columns or pretense in the plain
International style?

MICRO-CIVILITIES: A LITTLE LEAVEN

At the Interstate rest stop between
Clanton and the Magic City infamous

for hoses and police dogs, a heavy-set
black man in dark pants and gray pullover

leans his head on his arm against
the partition between our latrines as

we relieve ourselves—his breath rasping
and labored. Later he stands at the front door

with his back against the jamb and his
right arm flung wide to hold the stiff door

as a medley of men, women, children
from a dozen states crowd toward their cars.

After he nods me through and I catch
the door to release him from his Southern

hospitality trap, he says thanks, and walks
into the bright afternoon sun.

Micro-Civilities (II)

Dogwoods shade crimson, maples turn
gold, as I walk down 10th toward the park.
At the Foxx house, a familiar voice calls

from the yard. It is John, who is black
and whose name is White, a man of
wide talents who, his sign says, does

lawn care, janitorial work, painting,
and home remodeling. He once moved
my 95-year-old mother-in-law from

her home to Riverside Assisted Living.
Generous and perhaps schooled in psychology,
he compliments me for walking, and we

joke that in his line of work he doesn't
need more steps. Two brothers and a sister
had COVID, he says, and one brother died.

As I move south toward the park, his
whizzing Weed-Eater revs up, slicing
a neat edge beside late-blooming azaleas.

MICRO-CIVILITIES (III)

At Classic Car Care as they wash
my ten-year-old gray microvan
and I sit outside on a bench and read
All the King's Men again about how
power infects and ultimately implodes
the best intentions,
                        a tall, lean man
with weathered bronze skin, in gray satin
sweats and maroon shirt, approaches,
extends his hand and says, "I'm Bill.
Is this your car?"
                         Disavowing
the bright red Camaro parked near me,
I stand, shake his hand, and he wishes
me a good day, climbs into a tall
white pickup, and drives away.
                            Three
minutes, tops, and the day is warmer,
brighter.

Micro-Civilities (IV)

Headed home in summer heat after
looping the park—4,187 steps on
a good day, 2.21 miles—I notice

a gang of workers at the house of the
architect who loves wood and never
stops improving his place. Just ahead,

a painter in spattered pants and a
t-shirt that doesn't quite cover
his large white belly crosses the street

toward a dented and scraped pickup,
rummaging in a cooler in the back.
As I move past the truck, resisting

the urge to read the backwards ball cap
and pale skin as the wrong vote in
all recent elections—feeling I have seen

this book many times before and know
its pages—the man pulls a bottle from
the cooler, holds it up, and says, "Sir,

would you like a water?" Chastened,
I take a deep draw of the cold liquid
and turn down Sherman toward home.

Diversity

Athletes and coaches, no surprise
there, all shades of black, brown,

off-white, beige, tan, sepia—but now
the clerk at the bull's-eye store

pointing my granddaughter and me
to earbuds, the mailman who was

my wife's student and always wants
me to tell her hello, the poised

and quiet young woman in my comp
class, a milestone, best writer and

highest grade. Postal clerk Tammy
who mails my Christmas box and

offers stamps. Ads for Buicks and
asthma meds on t.v. Weather

women and men, anchors for local
and national news, reporters ranging

the globe. Authors in my beloved
New Yorker. Dog trainers, beach

ads, featured artists, and a black
woman whiskey distiller in our

Southern magazine. Poet Laureate
in a Deep South state. Secretary

of State, Vice President, President
of the United States. Senators,

Members of Congress, Secretary
of Defense. A grandson's girlfriend

named for the Far East continent
coming daily to our house. Local city

councilman, police chief, finally
a district judge to fill a vacancy.

                         Still,

Northwest Town, across the tracks,
where the rec center was condemned.

Wild ads by the Governor attacking
race theory, critical thinking. Jails,

prisons across the nation, packed
with black inmates. Bristling resentment

of any new info, any fresh angle, on
human bondage in our country,

anger at any preference for admission
or employment. Police shootings, fear

of black men, shootings in churches.
Exposure of sham convictions in old

courts, exoneration of old inmates,
lives wasted in a cell.

                    Justice
like new software on an old machine,

a flood of mixed and messy data,
stretching, straining, threatening

to crash the antiquated system.

TAKING A STAND

> *statue* < L *stare*, to stand

Ten steps north of the Confederate monument,
also facing east, Lady Justice *stands*, cast
in tarnished copper, original to the first
courthouse in a county older than the state.

Erect, poised, draped in flowing robes,
she lifts high in her left hand the balanced
scales of justice—fairness, equal treatment
for all—and in her lowered right hand, sharp
point upturned, she holds justice's sword,
its power to pierce pretense and subterfuge,
probe motives, and hold all accountable.
Her classic features are composed, sure,
crowned with laurel for victory.
                              The eyes
are clear, open, not blinded. She sees all
alike, undistracted by color, custom,
prejudice, hate, unperturbed by rhetoric
or public clamor.
                              For all her grace,
she is intense, relentless. In the country's
deep Depression, on this site, she moved
a brave and fair-minded judge to sacrifice
his reputation and public career so nine
black teenagers locked inside a false rape
charge might be spared hasty and unjust
blame.
        To the Lady's left, just beyond the
long shadow of Johnny Reb in deep winter,
a historic marker honors her work with these
Scottsboro Boys, how with unwavering effort—
like Atlas slowly lifting rounded Earth—she
bent, ever so slightly, the arc of the universe.

Part V

Waking Up:
What We Saw

The Jig Is Up

1952

Wise, patient, kind, her name
rich as a glowing sunset, she

taught me how *subtly*
a consonant could be silent,

gave me Cinder the Cat, who saved
her family from a burning house—

guiding her second grade charges
through letters, numbers, song, dance,

as gentle and relaxed as a white-gloved
conductor picnicking in the park.

Did she feel no twinge, no pang
of doubt, discomfort, in the room

with corn seeds sprouting in plastic cups
on the window sill and large flowing

cursive ABCs modeling penmanship
on the blackboard—after "Alouette,"

"Row, Row, Row Your Boat," "Three
Blind Mice"—when we sang in

sharp unison, *"Jump, jump, jump,
Jim Crow, take a little turn, and
away we go, slide, slide, slide"?*

What had we in County School to do
with Daddy Rice's smut-faced jingle

in the Big City a century and more ago?
With what power did the ditty grow

a hundred verses, bounce across
an ocean to delight the fair-skinned

Motherland? With what nuance
and drive did it sink roots in so many

psyches, families, churches, crackpot
theories, cross-burning rallies—like

wild deep-rooted privet bursting
across yard and field and forest—

to bloom unchecked in the clarion
voices of our little classroom choir?

It's Systemic

We begin with chains,
trade, beatings, money,

a man, woman no more
than a hog or mule. We

keep the cage for
two centuries. And when

we are forced to open
the doors, we crack

the whip in black night,
laugh at the bewilderment,

song, dance, black-face,
then say they can't

live here, eat or study
there, only work for us.

We beat, hang, burn
the insolent. Meanwhile,

they gather, sing hymns,
flee north, west, east,

and the system changes

like a car with locked
steering making a curve.

It's (Not) Racial

< It *razza* < ?

When I was ten and the slender
teenager Ralph with handsome face
and latte skin told me he had a daughter
not yet two, I marveled at the chasm
between the two rows of cotton we picked.
He had his world, I mine.
                        The houses
we lived in were weathered gray, but
we knew black and white, status guarded
like cells in a Tuskegee jail—everybody
in his place.
                        We didn't know
race was something we made up—
a façade for tribe, clan, kind, class, old
as hunger and fear—the word itself
so dark and deep we still can't find
the first stakes driven to mark our own.

We didn't know the boxes we filed
people in were flimsy as cardboard
and would collapse in the first hard rain.

We didn't know we could gather at one
table, eat ham, greens, cracklin' bread,
smell the rank chitlins cooking, could
work side by side as clerks, lawyers,
bankers, teachers, join hands at an altar,
share children and grandchildren, laugh
and hug when we meet.
                        For a sleep-walking
ten-year-old, the Black Sea, the Caspian,
the Caucasus, might have been on Mars.
He didn't know that to escape the rutted
mazelike roads that gripped the county,
all he needed was wings.

It's Theory

< Gr *theōria*, a looking at,
    contemplation
  < IE base **dhāu-*, to see

In our complete King James world,
theory was limp, flimsy, thin as a
muscadine vine on a tall blackgum,
too slight to bear our weight.
                     It was
vaporous, like fog in October outside
the farm house, obscuring the barn
and chinaberry tree, chickens pecking
in dim and soggy light.
                     Theory
let us escape—an open hatch as Moses,
Abraham, Jonah sank in a rising sea
of science, a back door ajar as the
deadly data closed in on us.

We didn't know theory *looked*
intently at the facts, *contemplated*
connections until it *saw* clearly.
                     We
didn't know it was strong as ligaments
holding muscle to bone as we crossed
Gantt's Mill Road toward the cow lot
and nodded to Johnny Terrell in the
dark pickup.
               Had we but *looked*,
we would have *seen* the deference
our black neighbors showed us,
the way they lived in houses off
the road or in clusters like Wall Street,
how they worked as field laborers.

We would have wondered why
the bank teller or retail clerk at Rush

Davidson's clothing store was always
white, like our teachers, classmates
at County School, the waitress at Snake
Baker's hamburger place where I watched
Yankees games on Saturday afternoons.

We would have known *theory* is as
real as the thick rope dangling from
a tall sycamore over Calebee Creek
that we swung outward on, its tight-
woven fibers as strong as the tree's
dense wood,
                        till we let go
and splashed into the cold current where
not a single black child appeared
in the laughing crowd.

It's Critical

critic < Gr *krinein,* to separate, discern
        < IE **(s)krei-,* to sift,
        < base **(s)ker-,* to cut

We *sifted* King James verses as fine
as the flour my father made biscuits with
every morning
                knowing on some night
when the moon stood blood red, people
would moan and shriek, be flung right
and left
                like the hulls of dried peas
beaten in a burlap bag, then blown by a
winnowing wind, chaff finally separated
from the good seed.
                And we could
discern the seasons for planting cotton
by mid-April, picking in late August,
and killing hogs after a November freeze
gripped the bare farm.
                But in all matters
black and white, habit and custom lay
on us like a stack of thick quilts in
the cold farmhouse, paralyzing, stifling
all thought.
                For all our vaunted verses,
we could not *separate* the ways of our
Southern fathers from God's ways—
could not *cut through* the dense and
hardened façade that said we were
poor but white.
                Lacking eyes to see,
ears to hear, hearts to know that our
happily plotted land lay under judgment,
we did not know we waited—while
lightning in the north promised rain
in one more day—for the storm to break.

It's Racial: Sticks and Stones

Words, it turns out, do hurt,
bruise, lacerate like a whip—
ugly, fat, retard, racist. We

wince, cringe against their
biting edge, resist such claims
of what we *are.*

        Our motives
are pure, we say, and wave
the flag of good intent.

          But
deep below the avid avowal,
where the mind moves before

we say what and why—
the uneasy conscience stirs
against the names we use,

jokes we tell, a tone we take
when we say the niece's new
teacher says *poe* for poor and

doe for door and report the
rumor that new mail carriers
in the city can't read properly

and are packing letters into
wrong boxes.
        The roads we

ride were laid long before we
breathed our first and cried out
on the world, schools were sorted,

neighborhoods platted and fixed,
fountains and doors clearly labeled,
gestures and glances as deeply

coded as acorns on an oak. We
lived on a farm we did not own,
our happy minds framed like a

sunlit park we played and worked
and ate and slept in—and from
our unthinking hearts now flow

words and deeds no mere hand-
washing can cleanse.
                          Can we

bear the shock of waking up and
facing neighbors we have failed?

It's a Choice: E-motion

In all the simmering cauldron
of our hearts, two feelings move us.

1
< IE base *leubh-, to be fond of, desire

Love is open, turns toward others,
leans in, drawn by arms spread
for embrace, by the tears or hunger
of one who needs what we can give.
Love feels others' grief, their loneliness.
It does not back away from scowls,
threats, or anger. Love wants what it sees,
takes it in—joy, hurt, and all.

2
< IE base *per-, to try, risk, come over

Fear floods over us, pulls us back,
judges, slams the door, turns away,
flees, trusting no one outside the tribe.
It cloaks itself in anger, hate, and pride,
pushes, lashes out, strikes, stabs,
shoots. Fear craves power—to subdue,
possess, lock others away. It never
has enough guards, never sheds worry,
never sleeps without alarm.

Greed and Grace

    < IE *ĝher, to crave
   > Gk *charis*, grace, favor

If we dig past the layers
of *greed*, what we crave and
yearn for—coins piled so high
we cannot spend them all, a house
with more rooms than we can
eat and sleep in, dark-eyed models
in the lingerie ad who might
lie beside us, keep us warm—

we find a spring, clear, bubbling
beyond all we can drink, welling up
over feet, knees, thighs, till we
splash, swim, dive, our ageing
body at ease, buoyed with joy
and gratitude.
         It is *charis*,
fountain of everything good,
always more than enough.
Blocked, hoarded, it sinks
slowly into itself, disappears.
Open to friend and foe, it
brims past all want, waters
olive, apple, pine, palm,
the towering trunk and hanging
fruit of the baobab tree.

We the People

constitute < *com-*, together
  + *statuere* < pp of *stare*, to stand

With Adams, Jefferson, Franklin,
Hancock, we pledge our lives, our fortunes,
our sacred honor, and *constitute* ourselves
one nation. We *stand together*, a union
not yet or ever perfect, a body, corporate,
indivisible, out of many, one. We claim
the creator's stamp, nature's equal rights.

But with these famous fathers we also
deem in law and practice some men are
not men but objects like lumber and livestock
to be sold, traded.
                    At the bloody
Pennsylvania battlefield where we killed
one another for dollars and pride, we stand
with Lincoln and dedicate ourselves to
a new birth of freedom for all equally,

and we confess our failure to respect
human worth and dignity in our neighbors.

Over his lifeless body we own decades,
generations of violence, intimidation,
fear-mongering, laws that bind and exclude,
custom rigid as the iron bars of a cage.

Standing or kneeling, hand over heart
or no, we bear *together* in our bones
two centuries of glory and shame—one
nation pledging anew liberty and justice
for all.

Epilogue:

Maybe This Time

Can habits clash like
cymbals in a band, oompah
from the tuba, wailing
tones of saxophone?
     And
do we dance in prancing
steps or boot stomping
squares?
     How many
decibels do we need? How
loud is too loud?
     What
time shall we keep, whose
clock strike the upbeat?

And who will frame the
feast we march toward—
will it be greens and yams?
chitlins? Carcass roasted
over open fire? Or some
crystal-pinging ritual carving
turkey in jacket and tie?

Is the house large, airy
enough for all, laughter
gathering in the rafters,
subsiding as we drift
toward sleep, humming
all the tunes we've heard?

Is this land that is our land
broad enough for all of us?
Is there music we can make
together?

HOPE

< ? same IE base as HOP

We hardly know where it starts—
gruel for starving lips, banquet
before battle—but it rises, leaps

up, springs like swelling buds
of dogwood, like a hungry tiger,
a quiet fountain flowing free—this

expectation of something good. If
it has feathers, it can soar and sing
at heaven's gate or cling unseen

to some perch only we know of.
It is possibility, trust, that good
things will come, bad will fade,

that with the sere leaf a seed will
drop—that bills will be paid, the
bleeding knuckle or shin will heal,

that strangers will treat us right, all
will value us, that justice will have
no price, no color, the son who

stumbles will find his way, words we
cast across the page will take a shape,
speak, and the world will listen. In

direst cold and wet, when all is dashed,
we hear the poet's wind-blown thrush
fluting unbidden across a dead century,

singing somehow of kindness and of joy
yet to come.

MAYBE THIS TIME

the yellow and black school bus
will stop at Herschel's house, and
he will get on and sit where he likes

and at the school where my mother
and uncle and brother went before me
the Governor will step aside and

shake Herschel's hand and welcome
him, and we will walk together to
a room where Mrs. Coan will teach us

wispy cirrus, layered stratus, towering
cumulus, and dark foreboding nimbus
clouds without alarm and to another room

where Mrs. Phillips will show us common
and proper nouns. Maybe this time Herschel
could play Jim in the operetta where I sing

Tom's whitewash lines. Maybe this time
Herschel will live next door to me and
we will throw the baseball together,

shoot hoops at the goal above the barn door,
and walk the half mile together for football
workouts in August. Maybe he'll take

Becky and I'll take Linda to the Mt. Vernon
Theatre beside the rusty water tower in
the town where Tecumseh incited the Creeks

and after seeing Tex Ritter and Lash LaRue
we can get burgers at the Sani-Freeze and hang
out laughing in the parking lot. Maybe we

will have classes together on the Plains. And
maybe this time they won't stop him because
he's walking or jogging or driving in some

neighborhood, and maybe he won't put his
hand in his pocket or have his hood up or
ask too many questions or lie down, and

maybe this time the officer won't put
his knee on Herschel's neck or draw his gun,
and even if he does, maybe this time, even if

Herschel runs, the officer won't fire.

Notes

"Birds of a Feather": For further information on the Tuskegee Airmen, see https://www.nps.gov/museum/exhibits/tuskegee/airwar.htm.

"Herman Shaw (I)" and "Herman Shaw (II)": For further information on Herman Shaw, see https://www.baltimoresun.com/news/bs-xpm-1997-08-24-1997236123-story.html and https://www.findagrave.com/memorial/66664911/herman-shaw.

"Confession: Only in Remembering": For more on the president's apology, see https://www.c-span.org/video/?c4584112/bill-clinton-apologizes-tuskegee-experiment.

For a detailed narrative and analysis of the Tuskegee Syphilis Study, see Fred D. Gray, *The Tuskegee Syphilis Study*, NewSouth Books, 1998, 2013.

"The Town": For background on the Tuskegee Confederate monument, see https://www.al.com/news/2018/08/tuskegee_confederate_monument.html.

"By Any Other Name," "What's in a Name? (I)," and "What's in a Name? (II)": "What's in a name? That which we call a rose / By any other name would smell as sweet" (Shakespeare, *Romeo and Juliet*, 2.2.43-44).

Information and almost all the language of "Isham's Will" and "Inventory: Ransom's Estate" are taken from actual legal documents.

"Ghosts (I)" and "Ghosts (II)", epigraph": "*Fieri facias* (abbreviated *fi.fa.*) is a Latin phrase that refers to a writ of execution which directs a state specified officer, usually a sheriff, to take control of a piece of property and sell it in order to satisfy the owner's debt or tax obligations" (https://www.law.cornell.edu/wex/fieri_facias).

"Man-Price": "Owe no man any thing, but to love one another: for he that loveth another hath fulfilled the law" (Romans 13:8, KJV).

"A New Earth: 1955": "But the day of the Lord will come as a thief in the night; in the which the heavens shall pass away with a great noise, and the elements shall melt with fervent heat, the earth also and the works that are therein shall be burned up. *** Nevertheless we, according to his promise, look for new heavens and a new earth, wherein dwelleth righteousness" (2 Peter 3:10-13, KJV).

"Just Some Human Sleep": "Were he not gone, / The woodchuck could say whether it's like his / Long sleep, as I describe its coming on, / Or just some human sleep" (Robert Frost, "After Apple-Picking").

"Revive Us Again": Title taken from old hymn by William P. Mackay: "Revive us again; / Fill each heart with Thy love; / May each soul be rekindled / With fire from above." For full text, see https://library.timelesstruths.org/music/Revive_Us_Again/.

"Members Only": "For the body is not one member, but many. If the foot shall say, Because I am not the hand, I am not of the body; is it therefore not of the body? And if the ear shall say, because I am not the eye, I am not of the body; is it therefore not of the body? *** But now are they many members, yet but one body" (I Corinthians 12:14-16, 20, KJV).

"Taking a Stand": For background on the Scottsboro Boys, see https://www.pbs. org/wgbh/americanexperience/features/scottsboro-boys-who-were-the-boys/ , and for a timeline of their trials, see https://www.pbs.org/wgbh/americanexperience/ features/scottsboronine-black-youth-arrested-for-assault/.

"It's Critical": "When ye see a cloud rise out of the west, straightway ye say, 'There cometh a shower; and so it is.' And when ye see the south wind blow, ye say, 'There will be heat; and it cometh to pass.' Ye hypocrites, ye can discern the face of the sky and of the earth; but how is it that ye do not discern this time?" (Luke 12:54-56, KJV)

"It's Racial: Sticks and Stones": "And Jesus said, 'those things which proceed out of the mouth come forth from the heart: and they defile the man. For out of the heart proceed evil thoughts, murders, adulteries, fornications, thefts, false witness, blasphemies: These are the things which defile a man: but to eat with unwashen hands defileth not a man'" (Matthew 15: 1-2, 16-20, KJV).

"Greed and Grace": "With its distinctive silhouette, broad trunk, unusual root-like branches, and large, velvety fruit, baobab is the best known of all African trees. The tree is steeped in legend, and due to the many different uses of its various parts, it is known by the local people as the 'tree of life.' A large tree can hold up to 4,500 liters of water; its fibrous bark can be used for rope and cloth; its edible leaves and fruit can provide relief from sickness; and its hollow trunk can provide shelter for as many as 40 people. So, it is easy to see why it has earned this name." (American Botanical Council, https://www.herbalgram.org/resources/herbalgram/ issues/108/table-of-contents/hg108-feat-baobab/)

"Hope": Echoes in the poem are of course deliberate. Pope: "Hope springs eternal in the human breast, / Man never is, but is to be, blest." Dickinson: "Hope is the thing with feathers." Hardy's "The Darkling Thrush": "I could think there trembled through / His happy good-night air / Some blessed Hope, whereof he knew / And I was unaware." Also phrases from Shakespeare and Shelley.

Acknowledgments

My thanks to the following publications, in which poems in this collection also appeared.

Anglican Theological Review: "Greed and Grace"

Bearing the Farm Away (Kelsay Books, 2018): "Fathers and Sons," "Isham's Will," "Inventory: Ransom's Estate," "Why GP Cries"

Beyond Paradise: The Unweeded Garden (Main Street Rag, 2020): "Greed and Grace"

Broken and Blended: Love's Alchemy (Kelsay Books, 2021): "Hands (I)"

Poets' Choice. Huntsville Literary Association: "Birds of a Feather" and "Hope"

Ponder Review: "A New Earth: 1955"

Swampland.com: "Why GP Cries"

Teaching English in the Two-Year College: "Fathers and Sons." Copyright by National Council of Teachers of English. Printed by permission.

Webster's New World College Dictionary, 4th ed.: All word histories are from this edition.

What He Would Call Them: "Why GP Cries" and "Fathers and Sons"

About the Author

Recipient of the 2014 Writers Exchange Award from Poets & Writers, Harry Moore is the author of the poetry collections *Bearing the Farm Away* (Kelsay Books, 2018) and *Broken and Blended: Love's Alchemy* (Kelsay Books, 2021), along with four chapbooks: *What He Would Call Them* (Finishing Line Press, 2013); *Time's Fool: Love Poems* (Mule on a Ferris Wheel Press, 2014); *Retreat: A Way Forward* (Finishing Line Press, 2017); and *Beyond Paradise: The Unweeded Garden* (Main Street Rag, 2020).

His poems have appeared in *Sow's Ear Poetry Review, Plainsongs, Xavier Review, Pudding Magazine, Slipstream, Main Street Rag, South Carolina Review, Blue Unicorn, Ponder Review, Anglican Theological Review, Pensive,* and other journals.

Retired after teaching writing and literature for four decades in Alabama community colleges, he lives with his wife, Cassandra, in Decatur, Alabama. More info at harryvmoore.com.